# Po
# Panda



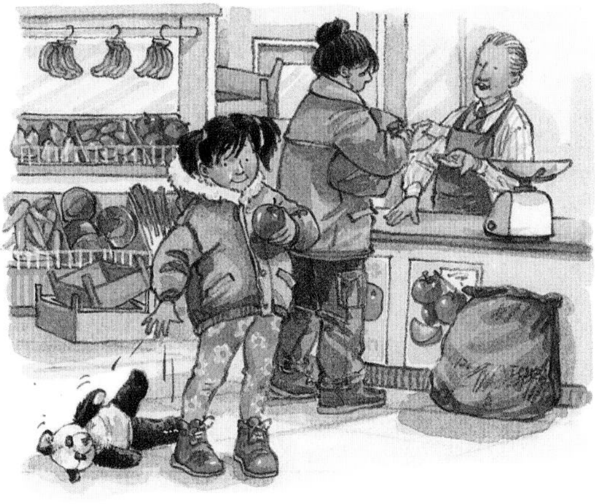

**Teresa Heapy**
**Illustrated by Shelagh McNicholas**

Rigby®
A Harcourt Achieve Imprint

www.Rigby.com
1-800-531-5015

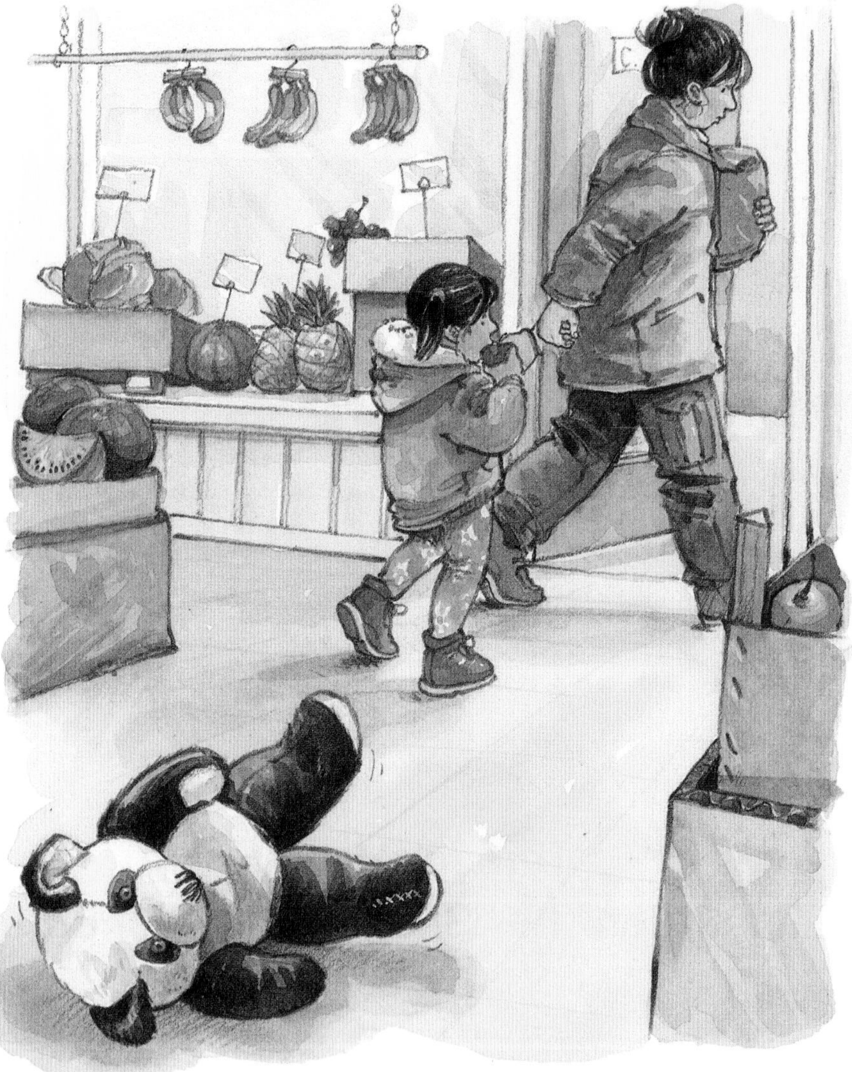

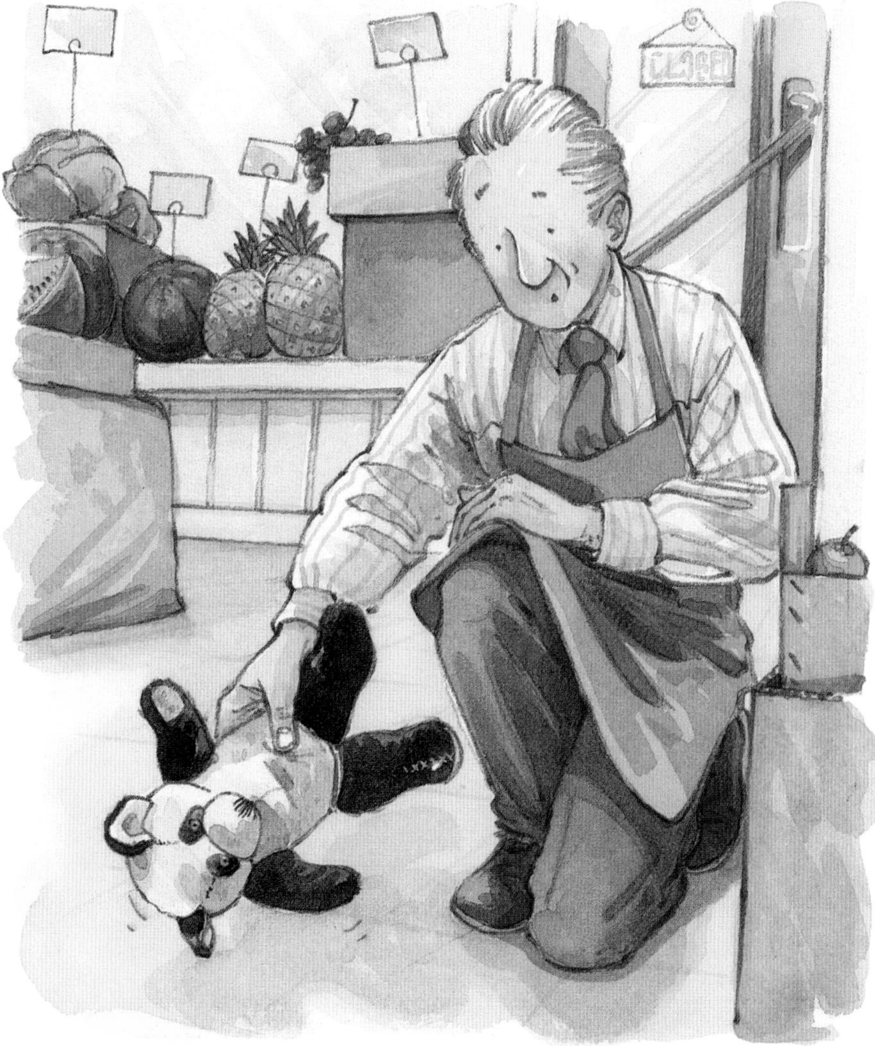
CLOSED

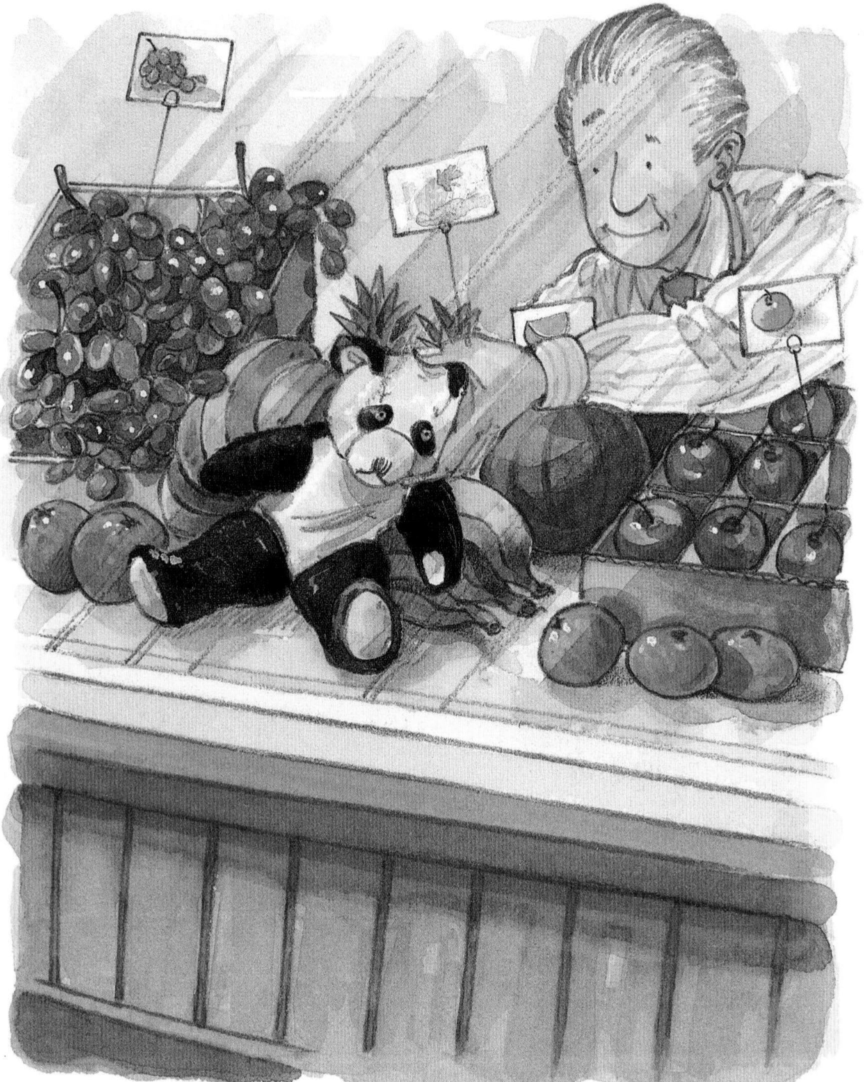

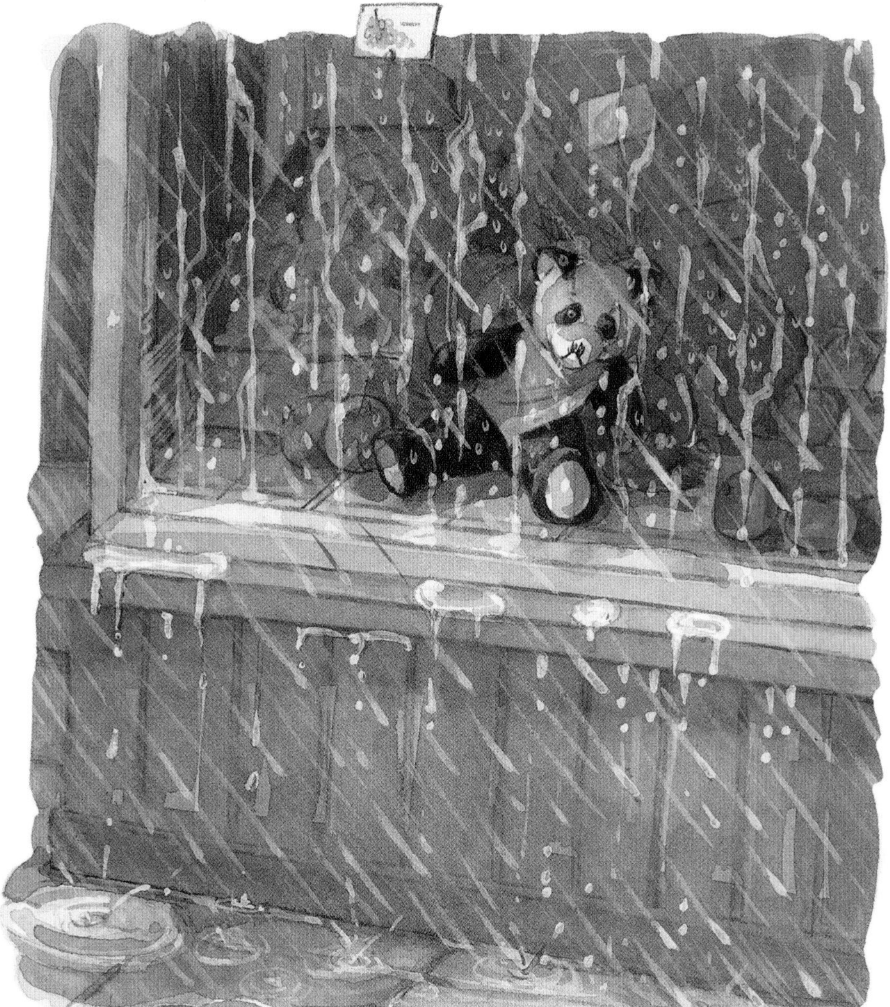

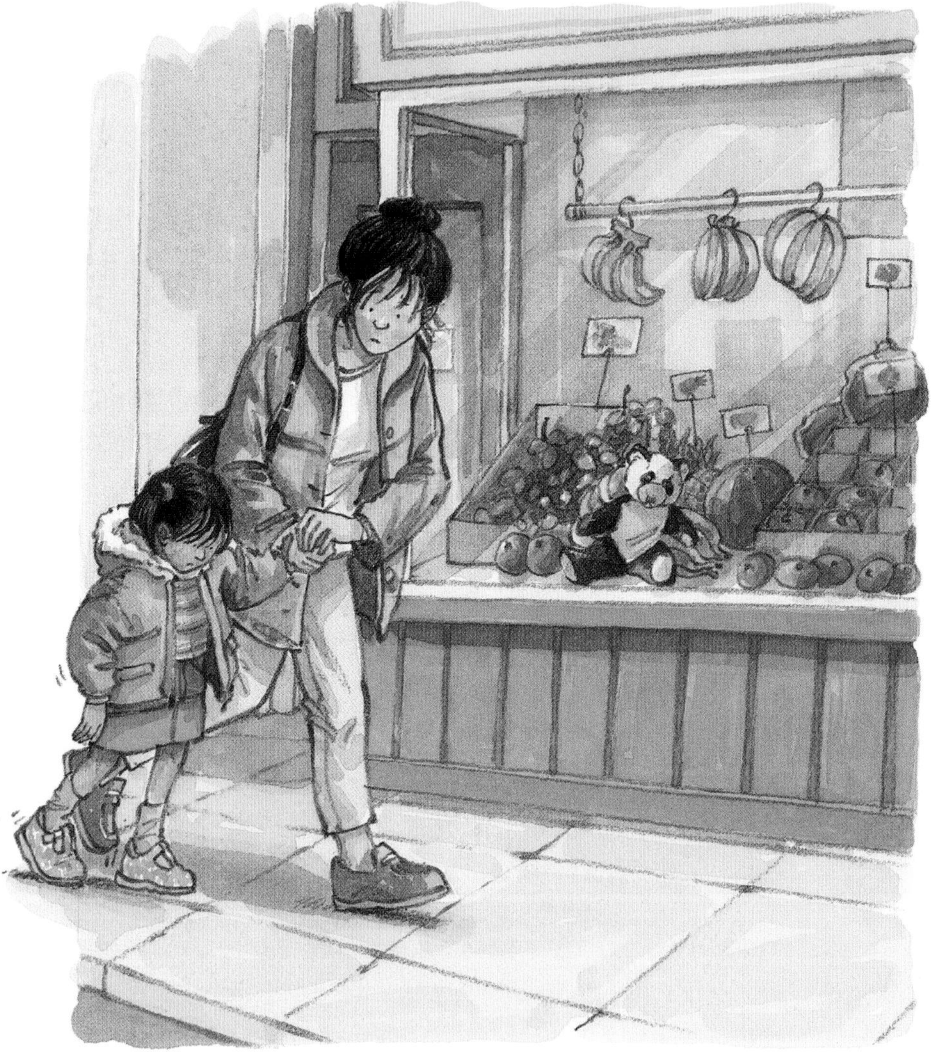

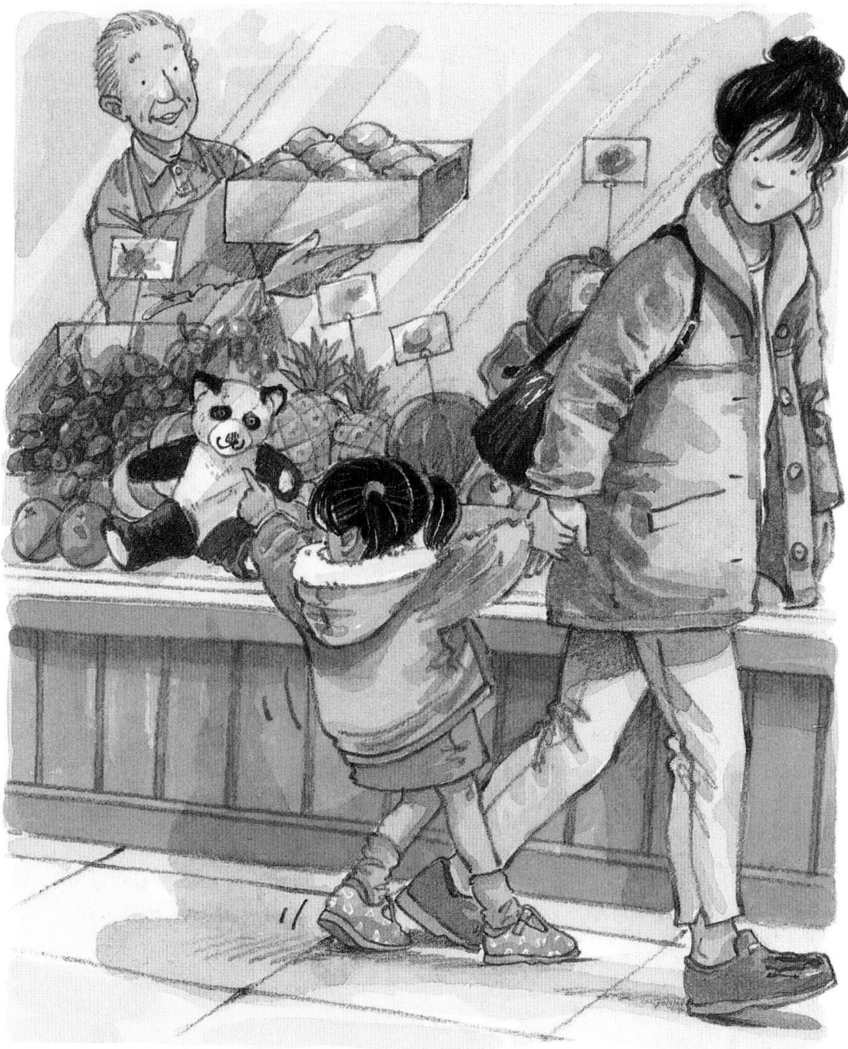

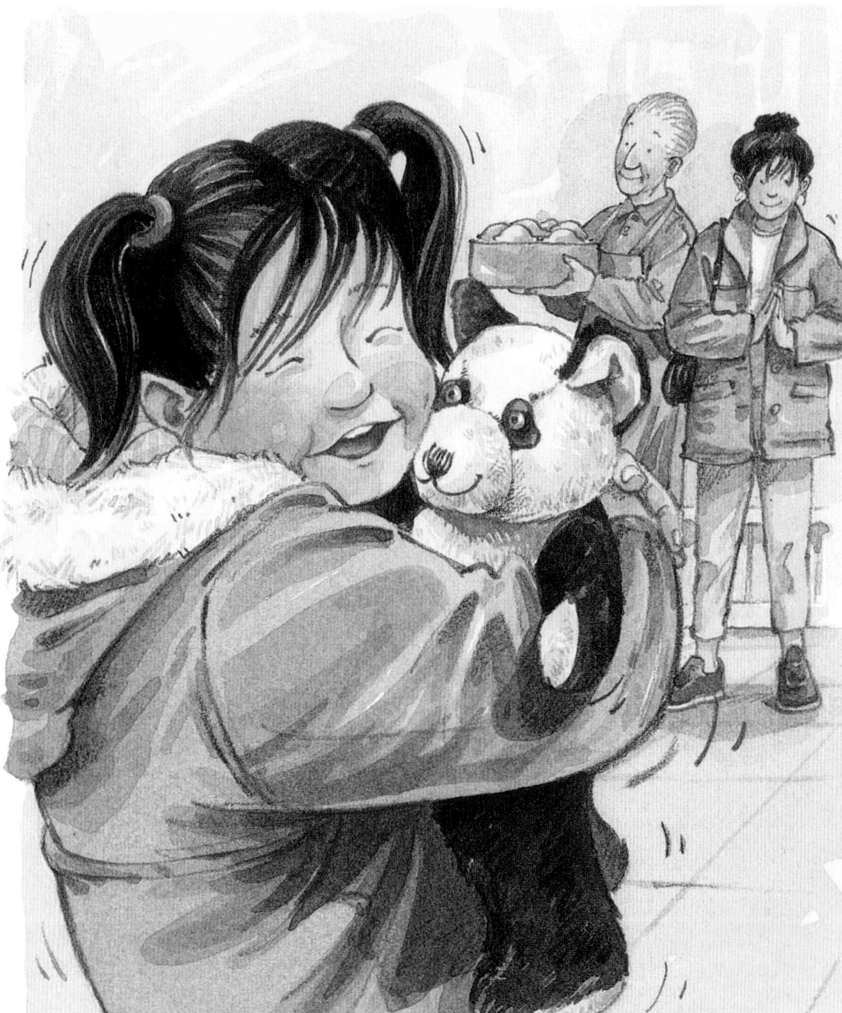